T0151049

A MINUTE WITHOUT DANGER

A Minute without Danger

Jacqueline Waters

Adventures in Poetry

Some of these poems appeared previously in the following journals:
The Germ, The Hat, Sal Mimeo

Cover design by Paula Wood
Typography and book design by *typeslowly*

Adventures in Poetry titles are distributed through Zephyr Press by
Consortium Book Sales and Distribution
www.cbsd.com
&
SPD: Small Press Distribution
www.spdbooks.org

9 8 7 6 5 4 3 2 FIRST PRINTING

ADVENTURES IN POETRY

NEW YORK   BOSTON

WWW.ADVENTURESINPOETRY.COM

ISBN 0-9706250-3-0

Contents

No News Is   11

Triangulated   13

White Zombie   15

John Donne   18

Figure   19

And It Came to Pass (Not to Stay)   20

The Haircut   21

Channeled   23

Telescopic   25

The Most Difficult Clock   26

Ghost   28

It's Like This   30

Invited — but Where?   32

Poem with Brightness and Contrast   35

Cars of the Future   36

I'm Not Listening   37

The Brain Trust   38

Matter   40

Basic History of the United States   41

White   46

On to Them   47

Hawaii   49

Essential Logic   50

Being   52

The Milos Line   53

Moving to the Tiny Port   54

Thought   55

A Minute without Danger   56

Forest   57

Make Use   58

Audio Drama   60

The Deserted Village of Feltville   62

A Minute without Danger

No News Is

There are several ways out of this. There's the spillway.
A tap at the valve, and winter softly
unloads a spring.
I fault no one. It was my limb.
I went out on it.
The severing was startling
like a hail of fumes from the sky.
But grief is mastery
of what was always wrong
and this is the psyche — a castle one passes,
admires, meets a few of the occupants,
attends a dance or dinner, helps put out a fire,
is robbed or mocked or sated,
leaves, finally, having to admit
that it was not a true experience.
For though consistencies exist
and opinions may be formed, judgment
can never really fall.
So the present is allowed to be The Age of Wonders.
Now the envious are the greatest among us
for to them some dull thing must speak
unimpeded in a heavenly way,
while most of us, under duress,

learn not to trust what we hear,
then to trust it, and then not,
dwindling as the universe expands.
After loss some yearning is customary
and dependable, even adorable
like the animosity between cats and dogs.
More eschewable is the sheepish moment
when moonlight penetrates the treehouse
exposing us for sentimental loons. Oh, can't we stay
and reminisce a while? No, our passage
has been arranged, a slight pressure
on the eardrums spurs our departure
though nothing's really certain till we pull in the ladder.

Triangulated

Wind out of the cardinal direction, surf fluctuating
Cabanas of green and white
Absorb all visible light

Let me pay out more line
A slight regret or scruple
Anxious to be compressed

We shiver like the day has no top
Plan to have fewer hang-ups, more laughs
People are not part of the plan

*

Time having just enough mass to move
Suspended from the lashings of the poles
Always on the side of accident

It's like my whole life never happened
Without sounding the words or scoring their values
Music lurking in another room that's

Permanently on the edge of pertaining
Lightly matted to thunder
A whisper drawn through a straw

＊

We pause like commas in the uproar
We have little interest in changing the system
Evidently we should all shut up

Just as standing still
Is mitigated by looking away
So the march of full stops

Littering this page and others
Oh it's a story something to charm them
In the interval between waking and rising

White Zombie

I cannot choose one or the other: I am like the fork.
The sky at the end of the powerline
withers away in shadow.
I retrieve the newspaper
conscious of my pajamas
and return up the driveway.
These beginnings embarrass me.
Like when I learned to play the pan flute —
I thought if I cultivated self-control
I would have an interesting, useful life...
Now I don't get out much, edge from room to room
peeking through the sashes, blunting urges.
I climb a ladder to clear a gutter
somehow knocking down a nest
of a perfectly comfortable family of wasps.
I am merely doing my duty, *but find I disturb others.*

When I was a child
but I was never a child
just as my boots had no life
until I put them on this morning.
Perhaps I ought to louver that elephantine window.
Or the hut entrance where the wax plants wax.

Then I saw a copy of the original
in the living room across the street
making me aware that I am not alone
that others are watching
from their beveled jewels and horns.
Let's back up a second.
A house must reflect the soul
with castle-sized door knockers
activity in the pantry
walls that leap to the hands...
I see I am moving away from my object
but in order to contemplate it I must miniaturize it
its circuits crossing the card and lighting,
falling dark by evening.
Look at the lights. Where's all that juice coming from?
There's not a station around here for miles.
Someone had better make it their business to see about that.
All along I've been changing the details
stuffing the book
with anecdotes of the poodle
high above the marbled bath. . .
I wasn't sure what to forecast
it was the noon of life
a moment of choosing.

Many trees grew tall and turned to signage
but I never forgot the future,
even now I proceed painstakingly toward it in stockinged feet.
I admire your fierce leaning on it.
Really? It's all due to an editing error.
I guess there are options, the things that crazy people
cling to, and there is later to think it over,
now to do it, if only in the sense
of backing up against it, sinking into it,
dying a little. You, at your most festive, barely quiver.
I reach over in my sleep and pour the water on the floor.

John Donne

Everybody is dead,
flowering quietly by a tree
through the long accelerating spring,
which distracts them, leaving others free
to open a club, whereas

at home, puzzling of an evening,
the mind launders the little desires,
and they turn out beautifully. We are also
talking to each other with no breath
which is nothing, but now
I'm afraid we've got to shelve everything
or be condemned to divide it. Let us pray.

The new world is a carpet, cut to pattern
and unrolled over the old, its freshness
as heavy as darkness
rolling over us. We believe an idea
that has been hooked but not yet landed,
unless handled adroitly,
can poison all existence
much as a prayer
far along in its missing would do.

FIGURE

oh creepy in the garden
with dense waist and hatchet
tiptoeing to a door full of wind

you shouldn't put it
madly to the mad necks of the
airplanes in their awkward

adolescence, out on the tarmac
with little money and elfin, unless
you've seen them cheating
or moping around too much in the air

AND IT CAME TO PASS (NOT TO STAY)

I finish the drink and turn the glass over.
After that nothing happens.
Nobody slugs me or shoots at me or even
complains. The moons pass like gels
among the torch ginger.
I nearly understand "you"
then you move and the mounds of snow
fall open like a book.
Time wasted in capitol buildings.
The dome buckles
its enormous weight
draws in the supporting columns
as when an unendurable emotion
hits an inconsolable soul.
Best to forget, then follow
with another kind of forgetting.
Sometimes I sit in a chair and read a magazine.
What is life?
Ushering light from the hatches.
All signs look good
before the scheduled hour of nudging.

The Haircut

Having talked out of turn
I will not go to sleep
I don't have much to sleep about
The land is dark
I'm inclined to overlook it
for the pageantry of internal stimuli
or pelting the floor
with clumps of grass
A little off the top

A fine mess is triggered
whereby sayings can't be said anymore
Progress is rooted in deceit
and the best deceivers tremble
before the inner life

And the intrepid bodies who got to earth first?
We'll get them to leave
turning their places over to us
their true inheritors
and false placeholders

This is what I've worked for all my life
going back to bed and staying there
Am I my own delimiter?
Not precisely, but time rubs off on us
and the hill goes on, up
to no displayable avail

Channeled

She awoke with precision
as though sleep were a form of indecision

The independent-minded maid
poked open a package of figs

There were a lot, but not too many

It had been an unsettled year
poured out in large, ornamental tears
haunting the files under the guise of caution
then recovering in a dilapidated vale
Here it was worth continuing, she wanted to emphasize
making an effort not to divert her eyes
though her teeth made it difficult for her to speak

Having listened to her memory
all wrong but nearly right
she looked in the bag then cinched it
Never had the river been so low

Regrets vanish, having no assailant
Tons are brought to fruition
And the supple confront the firm

Nothing to lean on but thistles and briars
No more qualms, no more frustrations
No more incongruent caulk

TELESCOPIC

Astonishingly waves of light
do not require us as a medium.

Shapes emerge from other shapes:
the initially irregular cloud

converts to a hideaway bed.
The fronds of the basket palm

touch the Chinese wallpaper.
Attentiveness like this

attracts spies so we whisper.
Details are unimportant.

Romance must not be interrupted
even by urinating.

THE MOST DIFFICULT CLOCK

It is hiatus at first, and you ride the elevator
Reassured by your aptitude. Even the elevator
Would compliment you on your assimilation of rote,
Of the singular methodology of personhood mit machinehood.
Afternoons you nap at your table, masking your unconsciousness
With a calendar propped at the back of your head.
Concurrently, the tideporch is quiet, the phonograph crackles,
The central figure is deeply, incongruously warm. Morning
Is breaking properly in a place distinguished by its gray —
So wholly dissimilar to your own assemblage of gray.
At the junction where the trolley turns, a funny story is slapped
Out to the row houses, introducing the dresscutter
With the marble pallor, or the woman described as
Cancelled postage, aging, making the whole city cry,
As if crying could win you a paid vacation. Strolling out
Of the stores scot-free, banging on pots and pans,
We wondered why they took our money in that particular
Chinatown, why the wind barely suggested itself in the cracks,
Why the night air sat outstretched like a serving spoon of chopping broth,
Stinking even. It is you with your penchant for abstract boldness,
For forthright adventure, your desire to ride in the sketch
Of the equestrian statue on the file folder, the one you misfile
At some point every day. What are we to do with you?

In the pedestrian tunnel, the fantastic sensation of falling.
The directions were implacable. The great nonfiction
Is the terror of having to move.

GHOST

The legible word was "weary"
then he said come to me
with a plaid face

I tore through the city
on paper feet
as the burgeoning city
leaked color swiftly to the farmlands

and out by the vanishing point
the background opened
meaning everything or nothing

an assemblage of rods and cones
gleaming in the sunlight
organized to swoop up the inhabitants

I missed them, but I was a civil engineer
prepared for such emergencies

He met me in the road
kicking the gravel

We spoke at length
of unnameable events
then he departed

It's Like This

I've expected kidnappers all my life
It doesn't worry me but I'm afraid it does you
Perhaps you'll read the papers until I come back?
Just as reason is composed
Of tiny reflective surfaces
(And the willow you heap on the drive)
Isn't there something else to look at
Without the camera, as if to make
The leap of faith?
                          Timely clouds
Come east to block the sewage plant
This was how it was: our group
Came into the world through a hollow log
After us no one else could get through
We had a lovely time that first summer
Lodged in a ruin of bellflowers

I was often aware that something
Would be milled from me
That a product would be extracted
As I studied the difference between idle time
Which we steal, and leisure time
Which we earn

The *sphere*

Was the shape I dreamt of most
Though it couldn't always aid me
When first I escaped that milieu
I stared into the querulous window
And out again: in the stars
There's fire, in the fire, stars
Some kind of cusp sustains me
Making waiting my primary diversion
So when they get here, the kidnappers
Advise them of these procedures
(Saw-toothed wind, twigs and their fractions)
Help them handle a sensitive situation
Like you they have a job to do
Without a whole lot of elbowroom
I'll be OK, I've got some prescription cold medicine
And my dream of the sphere
If necessary I can hold out all night

Invited — but Where?

Just hearing the waves is relaxing
But I came into this store so I must want something
To shirk a task?
Or consider it penance, a circuitous route
to credit for time served
If only that branch would stop rapping at the window
or there were a hook to hang my lungs on
during this submersion

Odd I had to learn how to act natural
To look as innocent as a beaker
though less rigid or reproducible
I washed the notes from my hands
I wanted to see what I'd finally say
idling by the bags of ice…   .

But what else have I been doing
I understand what kinds of problems there can be
Our institutions are no good anymore
No good, and the British are coming
Carts pulled by camels ply the roads
Possibly they talk
but unremarkably —
they could be talking to anyone .

∗

What she revealed by leaving was a husk, an irking of space
She had that little victory
twisting a pinch of loam between her fingers
and following the thread of its argument
Even the unexpected rainstorm
was unpretentious and approachable

Perhaps there was uneasiness
as the wind lifted the mudflaps, providing her a peek
at two wheels spinning heartlessly
in a homely trough of snow

A spoon smacks a dish in the next resonating chamber
She took a handful from the nest, wedged herself
into a seat, began groggily to recount
her tale of a feathered test

Not another minute in the wristwatch
at which she gazed, emptying intent

∗

We're just going to get the germs off your food
and put you into a nice pantsuit

Moving refuse further off
in the declinate horizon

This is the damp ancient ground
on which people make their arrangements
feigning surprise
but revealing indifference

They lie frozen, their hair pulled back, their t-shirts large
She let them sleep for fifteen more minutes
Then they got the old heave ho

POEM WITH BRIGHTNESS AND CONTRAST

The dark outline of the mille feuille
in the window expresses "big doubt."
As the sun scatters needles
on the lake, campers collect their wits.
The afternoon is approaching, boxed
with four power-adjustable points
similar to those of a table
when it is a mesa.
                         People litter
for all the money in the world.
That is happiness.
Dispatching our superfluous days
through panes and over sills,
leaving the silhouettes unfinished,
like holes meant to be filled in later.

Cars of the Future

The taxi arrived. I became
a recluse and finished the
felt hat. The people from the
door-jamb roamed around

in their undisputed way
and when the display
was done, photocopied
everything in blue

transparencies. The breeze
squeezed between us.
I had glacial fear
until with a bang
we all felt lucky about
the cars and sun and
later, museums.

I'm Not Listening

Nice clothes, is that a set?
To which he answered go home young lady
The fun to be had here is not your fun.
The music turned and swore at him.
He danced precariously over to the fire escape
Where a hooded figure was breathing.
Have I hit my mark? he asked, hovering
Like a plum duck. With characteristic envy
She occluded him, and the crunch was cold and darned.
He fretted against the screen. Ensuing,
The foot frenzy filled the room like carbonated bourbon.
The drunks, dance cards dangling,
Debated internally. Uptown the rivers swelled
And the creeks met their banks
Then overran them. The guests tore through their plates
In a balancing act. Maids and goddesses flung frowns
From the pediment of the inflatable temple.
She stood atop a stele and spoke: You own this town!
Though mark my words you'll grimace and falter —
Common decency necessitates it, and I'm so young and miserable.
Errantly, I sing to you. Chaos will provide.
A wild, riotous life is the one I choose for myself
And for all who follow me.

The Brain Trust

Shuffling the batch of graphs
He hit the street
His face a cascade of faces
Seeking the oddly beautiful crimp
In the darkly sinister code
To decipher it out of existence

A little wind girdled the loganberries
Bringing them to the fore
Froze the movers in their parkas
And they were no help to him
On to Castle Clinton
Straining his eyes at the new tableaux
I am asleep, he thought
But he did not hear much cussing

There were saucers of foil
At his elbows and near his feet
Collecting the set of conditions
Greenish clouds settled into his collar
I am awake, he thought
Combing the air with his hands

He turned to the statue
But his instincts failed to surface
There must be some mistake, he cried
To the watchers around the harbor
Though their eyes were smiling
Their mouths refused to move
What he does or doesn't know
Will or won't destroy him
A staggering blast
Driving the air through his heart

MATTER

The arrival went off without a hitch,
of spring, of frankness
tying us pleasurably to the ground
as a stem or train ticket fetches
the best possible life
and how to live it. Then we leave
so things don't get perfect

I'd go along the river
with you, to study just one thing
though you contain all the indications
they argue about and elude
like wiry hay, when the hay comes

Basic History of the United States

Steel wool, carborundum, hammers and
copper chisels removed the patina.
The century, long and unresponsive,
has stacked the chairs on the tables
and turned out the lights.
It's the first leg of the new experience.
The tar pits are completely safe, and you have
very pretty fingers. Do you play the piano? I mean,
stirring the tea is all well and good, but what of the hot house,
the writhing vines, the flimsy uniforms and the answers
that need only be true while we answer?
That life happens at all times in a context we do not understand,
and that most of our actions go unexplained even among our-
      selves…
Squalls hissed up through vents in the marshes.
That's how long ago it was.
Not that long ago,
and to my knowledge no one ever asked
why. So we'll never know.
The grooved lake floods the lures
putting us and our floats in places
we'd rather not be, you and I.
A feeling of twinhood in the dunes.
The crab's walk to the pylon and off.

Memory makes luck
any kind of luck
glow so long it nearly clobbers us.

Originally, we eased ourselves into the plot,
wary of involving our wives and cats.
The folk dancing, the breathing through reeds,
these we did not find appealing.
But when even swimming's akin
to launching a counter-attack
brooding by the Delaware will have to do.
And when the army's not available to carry us
across the thousand-year-old bridge
on its millipedinous shoulders
we'll have no choice but to stand and defend
our redoubtable beliefs.
But now we're through for the day
and in some cases (mine for example) forever.
I quit my job at the glue factory,
and took up residence under the bridge.
Somewhere, higher than a building, the wind whistles
and there's more wiggle room,
fewer traditions to pummel, less dust to blow off.
For what has settled around us
is not dust, but the new. And new things,
we find, are not like the old.

Nowadays we're doing more
with less, with the ostensible goal
of one day doing everything with nothing.
Also, I'm looking for work so if you hear of anything…
In this room with a view of something
the lacquered tables rise
and tremble.
People pass by, inexorably important
while they are before us,
but they pass utterly.
A band of yellow light
moving up and down the wall
as if words weren't private enough.

By mid-July of 1899 Bay Head was swarming with cottagers
        and hotel visitors.
Twenty sneakboxes entered the regatta. Mrs. Clark and Miss Donaldson
helped with the receiving line and saw to the gristle sandwiches.
Outside, club burgees distinguished the masts of the speediest sailors.
Club members swallowed gin. All discussed Paris, growing
        helplessly animated
while listing the charms of the belle ville sur fleuve.
Yet all too soon it had to end,
and there is no indication
that worthwhile events of this kind
will ever happen again.

To survive we must temper our natural optimism
and on a cold, dark night
let not a glimmer of hope show through.
We have our work. Some of us have love.
The point is to keep moving
in a composition in which no two objects
are lit by the same source.

It's early yet. Van Buren is President.
I watch a crane hoist a skiff and set it down
like a lens. I'll go by the old school
and hit a few balls. I've always loved to count.
Explorers move to annex the Northwest Passage.
Storms beat them back
to the New York State Thruway.
Anyway, it's too late to change our minds about
the location. We're stuck in it.
Lustrous seconds tick. But there's still time
for the scissored sun
to free itself from that clutch of trees
and blow the lid off this whole operation.
We'll take a wait and see attitude, and attend to such affairs
as we can manage, given our limited national lunch break.
It's the best shot we've got.
I mean, do the math.

Addendum

OK, how much? I ask.
Much, you reply,
harmonizing with me.
We won't have our heroes forever.
One day we'll stop asking them questions
and just gawk at them.
A hard sort of hand glitters in the foyer.
Then we'll wonder who we ever were
and whether our problems were real
considering how they solved themselves
without our "help." As long as one is awake,
one is cataloguing pictures for the exhibition.
We could always throw a blanket
over the whole country, ignore the lumps
and hope nobody finds out.
She slowed long enough to explain,
"I'm going to see the flying machine,"
then rushed ahead, her long orange scarf flapping behind her.

WHITE

The meter registers
the spray, its
space all the sea
it casts on
spaces
     throw our arms up!
     the people listen
     from their posts
then they are asleep
in the light
breathing like looped rope

On to Them

Without a thought I undo the day's work
I walk into spaces and react to them
Bones and muscles are arranged first
before the dreadful hulk of the personality
You might not want this information
but could always carry it on consignment

I live in a state of some kind of something
without pencil or postage
Apologies for my inattention
I was watching a fool rush in
A most inglorious occupation
Try and you'll be reworded
condemned to sulk among boxes of documents
minus the time it took to borrow
someone's pen

The halls have their own share of worries
turning away from you
and in a building of this size we
may never meet again

No trouble, just setting a pace
My other fixation is winnowing
The onus is on us
to make our debris unique
the secret shrug
at the center of earnest entreaty

I wasn't expecting you either
The call was lost
Keeping up a hum
to ward off disparate noise
New pools accumulate
and people drink from the head of a pin

I could make a panel
a slim black box

To be as you were, accepting and unacceptable —
a shadow in the corridor
plunging lifelike into the folds
O degenerative, degenerative tale

HAWAII

Hey, forget about it. I was worlds away just then,
not quite set, a neutral trip to the market
for sandals and WD-40.
They say she who talks like a book
is tiresome to listen to,
though sometimes it's appropriate to talk like that.
Now everyone in the book is making fun of me.
Nor can I locate, as promised, the type
of violet card stock you needed
for the fraudulent health club i.d.,
while in Regensburg the heaps of leaves
accost the trees
demanding rapprochement.
Go easy on me. There's a lot
in my Cyrillic domed head
that I'm not proud of.

Essential Logic

By now I know all about respectable stupidity.
I invented it myself long ago,
with my family's full cooperation.
The dealership gave me a cushion,
and it was understood that eventually
I would join the force.
But the picture has a split-level appearance.
Internal Affairs declared worthlessness
a select quality, not to be claimed
by just any old artwork.
I spent weeks in the lab
producing a rebuttal: "I wouldn't say
the brain can be studied from the inside," I wrote.
"How smoking gun of you," they answered.
In fact, the nearer two arguments lie on a given
chromosome, the greater their chance
of being passed along as one.
This observation was rapidly confirmed
in many other organisms,
and soon they were peering over my shoulder at
not just the creation of a pattern,
but an examination of the principles behind a pattern.
Nonetheless, I abandoned the whole inquiry.

It was written only for lovers,
and it is well known that lovers find amusement
in highly inconsequential things.
This whole fucking country acts as though it
were about to be invaded by its own future —
as if the missing text were more important
in outline than in detailed exegesis.
I've ended up almost entirely friendless.
The only thing to guard against now
is friendship.

BEING

They're alone. No one has to
figure out the sequence:
fun will be along

to adjust the focus:
One moot thump
and gods, the wiliest

of pals, come peeking
out of books

tossing a ball about.
Without being entirely serious

the latent narrative
surfaces. It's newsy.

THE MILOS LINE

What I like about you
Is your economy. I'll take that
From you too, but first
Let's consider our affairs
As warm principalities
Plush with evergreens.
Youth is implausible —
Not wrong, but an imposition,
A winsome gesture, like a clue
In an uncrackable case.
The ship is lit with triangles.
Streamers flutter
From the distinguished class deck.
Shortly we leave Piraeus
Where the waiters are ruining our lives.

Moving to the Tiny Port

These are not unimportant parts
Without them we agree
The sky stripped down to the sea
When the wind begins to emulsify
In the southwest
                and responding
To this emergency, we hurl integers
Until the break becomes unbridgeable
And absorbing that succès de scandale
Climb the rocks, angling to disclose
The offshore trusts, as the fog banks
Around our deceptively tall town

Thought

There's that then there's trees
wafting over the investigation
next week's lamps and buoying words
going off for a swim in the sea

aren't we? past the heavy scenery
the violet waves proceed
the belt of stars
reflected in the waves

pleasing enough
but somewhat different, the playing fumes
too true or too hopeful
so we ought to stand and contemplate that

A Minute without Danger

I can't perform the operation
in ventilation like this. I have to run.
Come on, pretend it's the marathon
and we're all drunk. The cattails sway
indiscriminately along the turnpike
like hot little mitts. I was always on the road,
installing fiberglass, criminal minded.
It was just the furniture,
and I was an object — how pleasant
to be immobile. Inside the compartment
a stack of cards said *We've Moved*.
Nature is great: it forgot it was chaos.
And this morning the root of our troubles departed,
pushed itself right up out of the dirt
and through the freedom opening.
Is there freedom? It isn't the same window
that's repeated all over the world.
I like to call it tough luck
as if these windows almost (but never quite)
lead to the current events that will set the standard
for all future current events.
You have a huge brain
so I know you can appreciate that.

FOREST

This dim life. A trip to Hopatcong
but look away at the last instant
and brush in a parable. Night
is dumb light

a kind of raincoat
we'll believe the lessons when we can't
keep them off us anymore
the body with its plume

inconstant like a knee, moving roofs
to clearings, balancing the equation
with clods of earth, one is happy
or afraid, considering the world
with its squares going by

Make Use

The afternoon drifts from its soluble morning
The pistol blows unprovoked
Dunces plod onward with spiritus et animus
There's plenty to be angry about

Holding up a finger to stop the limousine
This is really happening
Or so I thought. Did I see it?

As I grew such need I had grew less
The same with the day
Flickering through the meridians
Adhering to the earth with dimming interest

And though turning back was unthinkable
Past conflicts and misunderstandings
Were important to resuscitate, get down to
Drive at

*

Silhouettes under a stone arcade
Double up to save fuel

Real attention is the sacrifice of imagining
Is it half-right that by a whole I mean a string
I'll let you get on with your life

Reading and writing have their place
Uninterested in observation
I needed help with the naming
A shade was flapping and I leashed it
This was character as I learned to have it

Revealing an urgency to seize that moment
Which was but one in a list of them —
Strange that desire to maintain the past
To go right up to it, surveying the damage

It's only looking, or maybe it's knowing
And I'll probably die doing this
Rising with the sap every season
Alarmed yet unalarmed
With the craning going on in all quarters

Audio Drama

I can help you, but you'll have to do as I say.
By the spring of 1975 a map of the world
appeared on a huge hand that
came out of the sea and touched the sky,
causing us to become similar.
In fact you were like a mirror
but only in the irritating sense that I
could not forget myself while I looked at you.
But life was mostly gripping.
The neighbors came out to collect the debris
drifting down from space.
In the evenings we read joke books —
jokes about germs and feet and meters,
then one more big joke to top the others.
Often it ended in a discussion of something personal.
You had your collection of barn hexes.
I led you to understand that true happiness exists
only during the reversal of true unhappiness
which we repeated like an old truism.
And so it was that I lived all these years without a memory,
while you felt yourself on the verge of recognizing
nearly every face you saw.
Luckily amnesia has been brought to this country

to offer us something better. Sign here
and initial here and here.
Forty hours a week spent walking upright
until one day it just took.

THE DESERTED VILLAGE OF FELTVILLE

I am served a cold puff
It does little to dispel the clouds
over fields created by the removal of trees
ballooning out of context
The abandoned mill is a hazard
Ruts are readied for the automobile
What came passing by, each clock ticking
The inutility of my head in the rain
But what's the attraction?
Being valuable though having no pelt
I roll my window up
They'll introduce themselves to me but
otherwise won't speak
Luminous peering, mentally checked off
We walk the streets at night freely
but now fatigue and cynicism are setting in
The rooms had knots that slid
They sold it off a foot at a time
They were totally crazy about the idea
Is there another place in the country
better equipped to keep the mind pliant?
The famously belligerent litany of attractions
The brochure was flying out the door

I could only get to the end of the road and back
I wasn't shouting anymore
The limestone was very loose, very salty
I flapped in the wind like one of those invitations
Page, edge of page, then the plummet
to warm and stretch the hands
preparing them for conversation
Despair made a few passes
found little to attach, and was tucked away
I saw into the future as far as retribution, no further
He inched over to amuse me
I stood unamused
Yet visitors weren't important
Their honey-eyed boots and vague spaces
The table laden with blobs and saucers
They'll come for me one day
claiming a spot on the river, throwing caution to the dogs
This was some power
You had to laugh
Thanks to honesty, I was a nervous wreck
The worst instincts and the cheapest laughs
The alarms should have gone off
We tried another channel
They were stuck where their urgency put them
Walls and walls of debriefed blue stand-ins
each of us thrifty with courage